THE NATIONAL ANTHEM

A TRUE BOOK

by

Patricia Ryon Quiri

Children's Press®
A Division of Grolier Publishing

New York London Hong Kong Sydney
Danbury, Connecticut

The 1814
American flag

Reading Consultant
Linda Cornwell
*Learning Resource Consultant
Indiana Department
of Education*

*Author's Dedication
For my son Rob, who always
makes me smile
Love, Mom*

Visit Children's Press on the Internet at:
http://publishing.grolier.com

Library of Congress Cataloging-in-Publication Data

Quiri, Patricia Ryon.
    The national anthem / by Patricia Ryon Quiri.
        p.   cm. — (A true book)
    Includes bibliographical references and index.
    Summary: Describes how a patriotic and eloquent attorney was inspired
to write "The Star-Spangled Banner" after witnessing the British attack on
Fort McHenry during the War of 1812.
        ISBN 0-516-20625-7 (lib.bdg.)   0-516-26382-x (pbk.)
    1. Key, Francis Scott, 1779-1843—Juvenile literature. 2. United States—
History—War of 1812—Literature and the war—Juvenile literature. 3. Poets,
American—19th century—Biography—Juvenile literature. 4. Patriotic poetry,
American—Authorship—Juvenile literature. 5. Star-spangled banner
(Song)—Juvenile literature. [1. Star-spangled banner (Song) 2. United
States—History—War of 1812. 3. Key, Francis Scott, 1779-1843. 4. Poets,
American.] I. Title.   II. Series.
PS2167.S73Q57 1998
811' .2—dc21   97-10970
                                                                                      CIP
                                                                                       AC

Contents

A Song of Praise   5

A Problem with Great Britain   10

The War of 1812   16

Washington Burns   18

Fort McHenry   24

"The Star-Spangled Banner"   36

American Pride   41

To Find Out More   44

Important Words   46

Index   47

Meet the Author   48

American schoolchildren singing the national anthem

A Song of Praise

"The Star-Spangled Banner" is the national anthem of the United States. An anthem is a song of praise. The people of the United States sing "The Star-Spangled Banner" to show their pride in and love for their country.

"Star-Spangled Banner" is also a nickname for the flag of the United States. Other nicknames

Today, the American flag has fifty stars and thirteen stripes.

for the U.S. flag are "Old Glory" and the "Stars and Stripes."

Since 1960, the flag of the United States has had fifty stars and thirteen red and white stripes. The stripes stand for the thirteen original states. The stars stand for each state of the Union.

The United States has had many different flags during its history. The first official flag, adopted in 1777, had thirteen stars and thirteen stripes. In 1795, the flag was changed to

The first official American flag had thirteen stars and thirteen stripes.

fifteen stars and fifteen stripes. Vermont and Kentucky had just joined the Union, so a star and stripe were added to the flag for each of these states. This flag lasted for twenty-three years.

As the number of states grew, it became clear that the flag would become too big if more and more stripes were added. Congress then decided that the flag should always have thirteen stripes representing the original states, but that a star should be added each time a new state joined the Union.

From 1795 to 1818, the American flag had fifteen stars and fifteen stripes.

This flag with fifteen stripes would eventually inspire a young lawyer and poet named Francis Scott Key to write the poem that became our national anthem.

A Problem with Great Britain

The United States had won the Revolutionary War against Great Britain in 1783. The United States fought this war to gain independence, or freedom, from British rule. The young country was on its way to becoming prosperous. Goods

A Revolutionary
War battle

British ships trying to block
American ships in the early 1800s

were being shipped to other countries, and businesses were making a lot of money.

Britain, however, had been at war with France since 1793. In the early 1800s, Britain decided to stop U.S. goods from going to France. British officials began stopping and searching American merchant ships bound for France.

Worst of all, Britain claimed the right to remove British-born American sailors from American ships. The sailors were impressed—forced to work—on British warships. Between 1805 and 1812, more than six thousand American sailors were impressed, including many U.S. citizens "mistaken" for British subjects.

The British kidnapped American sailors and forced them to work on British warships.

The War of 1812

At that time, James Madison was president of the United States. The nation's capital had moved from Philadelphia to Washington, D.C., in 1800. Some parts of the White House—called the President's House in those days—were still being built. On June 18, 1812, President Madison

President
James Madison

signed a declaration of war
against Great Britain.

Some people called this war
"Mr. Madison's War." Many
Americans were unhappy about
the war, especially people living
in the Northeast. But Americans
living in the South and West
were in favor of it.

Washington Burns

Many land and sea battles were fought during the War of 1812. The British troops were well-trained. In August 1814, British troops marched into the capital city of Washington, D.C. Americans feared for their lives, and most people fled the city.

In August 1814, British soldiers invaded and burned Washington, D.C.

Dolley Madison

President Madison's wife, Dolley, refused to leave until it was absolutely necessary. She put a meal on the table for President Madison and his men in case they returned.

Then, at the last minute, she stuffed important papers, silver, and some draperies into her baggage. Before she left the President's House and fled

Dolley Madison rescuing the Declaration of Independence before fleeing the President's House

to safety, Dolley Madison managed to cut a famous portrait of George Washington from its frame. She was not going to allow the British to burn it.

The British stormed into the city and burned down many public buildings. When they reached the President's House, they ate the dinner Dolley had left for Mr. Madison and then burned the house to the ground.

British soldiers burned the President's House to the ground.

Fort McHenry

After burning the city of
Washington, the British
tried to take Baltimore. This
city was the fourth-largest
in the United States and an
important shipping center.
Baltimore was just across
the river from Washington.

The men, women, and
children of Baltimore

A view of Baltimore in the early 1800s

worked hard to protect their city. They dug trenches and built walls so that the British would have a hard time getting into the city. The only way the British could attack was by water. They would have to destroy Fort McHenry to take Baltimore.

Three days before the attack, Francis Scott Key, a young lawyer and poet from Georgetown, was allowed to board a British warship. President Madison had given him permission to do this. Key hoped to persuade the British to release an American prisoner named Dr. William Beanes.

Francis Scott Key (right) boarded a British warship (above), hoping to gain the release of an American prisoner.

The British did give up Dr. Beanes. But the two Americans had to wait on a small boat behind the British fleet until the battle for Fort McHenry was over.

The sea attack began early in the morning of September 13, 1814. As Francis Scott Key watched in horror, the battle raged for twenty-five hours. Rockets and bombs burst and exploded. The smoke was so thick that most

A distant view of the British attack on Fort McHenry

British ships bombarding Fort McHenry

of the time Key couldn't see the fort.

On the morning of September 14, the smoke cleared a bit. Key saw with delight that the U.S. flag still flew over Fort McHenry. The United States had won the battle! Key was so moved

After the battle, Key saw that the American flag still flew over Fort McHenry.

On the spot, Key wrote a poem to express his joy that the United States had won the battle.

that he wrote down his feel-
ings on a piece of paper he
found in his pocket. Little did

he know that his poem would eventually become his country's national anthem.

The Star-spangled banner.

O say! can you see by the dawn's early light
What so proudly we hail'd at the twilight's last gleaming,
Whose broad stripes and bright stars, through the clouds of the fight,
O'er the ramparts we watch'd were so gallantly streaming?
And the rocket's red glare - the bomb bursting in air
Gave proof through the night that our flag was still there?
O say, does that star-spangled banner yet wave
O'er the land of the free & the home of the brave? —

F S Key

Fort McHenry's Flag

The huge flag that flew over Fort McHenry was made by Mary Pickersgill, a woman from Baltimore. It weighed 200 pounds (90 kg) and measured 42 feet (13 m) long by 30 feet (9 m) wide. Each star was 2 feet (60 cm) across. This star-spangled banner was damaged during the attack on Fort McHenry, but in time, it was repaired. Today, you can see that flag at the Smithsonian Institution in Washington, D.C.

"The Star-Spangled Banner"

After the battle at Fort McHenry was over, Francis Scott Key finished his poem. The original poem had four verses. The next day, he had it printed under the title "The Defense of Fort McHenry." A note at the top of the poem

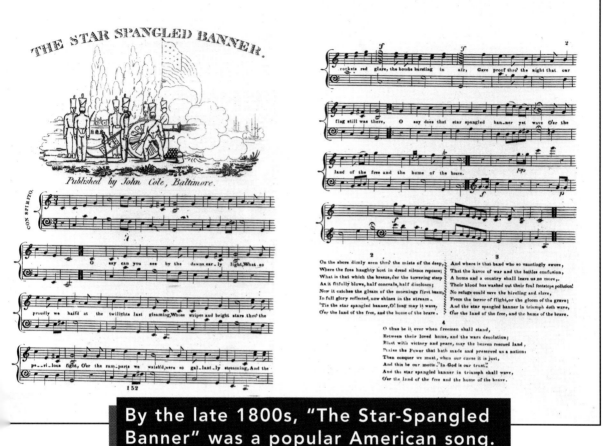

By the late 1800s, "The Star-Spangled Banner" was a popular American song.

said it should be sung to the tune "Anacreon in Heaven." This was a popular English drinking song.

By November 1814, the song had been published in Baltimore, and it was soon published in many other cities. In 1895, it was adopted by the U.S. Army. Soldiers began to sing it at the raising and lowering of the flag. Soon, everybody knew the melody and people all over the United States were singing it.

Finally, on March 3, 1931, 117 years after Francis Scott

H. R. 14

(PUBLIC....No....623....71st CONGRESS)

Seventy-first Congress of the United States of America;

At the Third Session,

Begun and held at the City of Washington on Monday, the first
day of December, one thousand nine hundred and thirty.

AN ACT

To make The Star-Spangled Banner the national anthem of the
United States of America.

---

*Be it enacted by the Senate and House of Representatives of the
United States of America in Congress assembled,* That the composi-
tion consisting of the words and music known as The Star-Spangled
Banner is designated the national anthem of the United States of
America.

Nicholas Longworth

Speaker of the House of Representatives.

Charles Curtis

Vice President of the United States and
President of the Senate.

Approved, March 3, 1931,

Herbert Hoover,

Key wrote it, "The Star-Spangled Banner" was made the national anthem of the United States.

"The Star-Spangled Banner"

O! say can you see
by the dawn's early light,
What so proudly we hailed
at the twilight's last gleaming?
Whose broad stripes and bright stars
through the perilous fight,
O'er the ramparts we watch'd,
were so gallantly streaming?
And the Rockets' red glare,
the Bombs bursting in air,
Gave proof through the night
that our Flag was still there.
O! say does that
   star-spangled
Banner yet wave,
O'er the Land of
   the free
and the home of
   the brave?

American Pride

"The Star-Spangled Banner" is played at all official occasions in the United States. It is also played at schools, before ballgames, and at the Olympic Games when a U.S. athlete wins a gold medal. Americans are proud of their anthem. They sing "The Star-

The national anthem is sung at all official government occasions.

Opera star Jessye Norman singing the national anthem at the 1996 Democratic National Convention

Spangled Banner" to show their respect for their flag and their loyalty to their country.

To Find Out More

Here are some additional resources to help you learn more about the national anthem:

 **Books**

Fradin, Dennis Brindell. **The Maryland Colony.** Children's Press, 1990.

Kent, Deborah. **The Star-Spangled Banner.** Children's Press, 1995.

Kroll, Steven. **By the Dawn's Early Light: The Story of the Star-Spangled Banner.** Scholastic, 1994.

Quiri, Patricia Ryon. **The American Flag.** Children's Press, 1998.

St. Pierre, Stephanie. **Our National Anthem.** Millbrook Press, 1992.

Whitcraft, Melissa. **Francis Scott Key**. Franklin Watts, 1994.

Organizations and Online Sites

Flags

http://www.law.uoknow.edu/flags.html

See various flags from U.S. history, as well as the official flags of all fifty states, territories, and possessions.

Flag of the United States of America

http://www.geocities.com/CapitolHill/4182/

History and timeline of the American flag with dozens of links to related sites, including state home pages.

Fort McHenry National Monument and Historic Shrine

East Fort Avenue
Baltimore, MD 21230

Features exhibits on the famous battle that inspired the song "The Star-Spangled Banner."

Important Words

anthem song of praise or loyalty

banner flag

declaration statement

gallantly bravely

gleaming shining

hailed saluted

harbors places where boats dock

o'er over

perilous dangerous

prosperous rich

ramparts walls of a fort

spangled covered with something sparkling

trenches ditches

twilight the time of day just before dark

Index

(**Boldface** page numbers
indicate illustrations.)

American sailors, 14, **15**
"Anacreon in Heaven"
   (song), 37
Baltimore, 24, **25,** 38
Beanes, William, 26, 28
British warships, 14, **15,**
   27, 30
burning of Washington,
   D.C., 18, **19, 23**
Congress, 8
"Defense of Fort McHenry,
   The" (poem), 36
flag, American, **2,** 5, 6,
   6, 7, **7,** 8, 9, **9, 31, 34**
Fort McHenry, 24, 26, 28,
   29, 30, 31, **31,** 35, 36
France, 13
Great Britain, 10, 17
Hoover, Herbert, 39
impressment, 14
Kentucky, 8
Key, Francis Scott, 9, 26,
   27, 28, 30, **31, 32,** 36, 38
Madison, Dolley, 20, **20,**
   21, 22

Madison, James, 16, **17,**
   20, 26
national anthem, **4,** 5, 9,
   33, 39, **42, 43**
Norman, Jessye, **43**
"Old Glory" (flag nick-
   name), 6
Olympic Games, 41
Pickersgill, Mary, 35
President's House, 16,
   22, **23**
Revolutionary War, 10, **11**
Smithsonian Institution, 35
"Stars and Stripes" (flag
   nickname), 6
"Star-Spangled Banner"
   (flag nickname), 35
"Star-Spangled Banner,
   The" (song), 5, 36, **37,**
   39, 40, 41
United States, 5, 6, 7,
   10, 24, 31, 38, 39, 41
U.S. Army, 38
Vermont, 8
War of 1812, 16, 18
Washington, George, 22
Washington, D.C., 16,
   18, **19,** 35
White House, 16

Meet the Author

Patricia Ryon Quiri lives in Palm Harbor, Florida, with her husband Bob and their three sons. Ms. Quiri is a graduate of Alfred University in upstate New York and has a B.A. in elementary education. She is a second-grade teacher in the Pinellas County school system. Other *True Books* by Ms. Quiri include *The Bald Eagle*, *The American Flag*, *Ellis Island*, and *The Statue of Liberty*.